Questions of Faith

QUESTIONS OF FAITH

A WORKBOOK COMPANION
TO THE CATECHISM OF
THE CATHOLIC CHURCH

MICHAEL AMODEI

ave maria press   Notre Dame, IN

Scripture texts in this work are taken from the *New American Bible with Revised New Testament and Revised Psalms* © 1991, 1986, and 1970 Confraternity of Christian Doctrine, Washington, D.C., and are used by permission of the copyright owner. All rights reserved. No part of the *New American Bible* may be reproduced in any form without permission in writing from the copyright owner.

Excerpts from the English translation of the *Catechism of the Catholic Church* for use in the United States of America copyright © 1994, United States Catholic Conference, Inc.—Libreria Editrice Vaticana. Used with permission.

Many of the quotations of saints were published in *Quotable Saints* by Ronda De Sola Chervin (Ann Arbor, MI: Servant Publications, 1992).

© 2000 by Ave Maria Press, Inc.

All rights reserved. No part of this book may be used or reproduced in any manner whatsoever, except in the case of reprints in the context of reviews, without written permission from Ave Maria Press, Inc., P.O. Box 428, Notre Dame, IN 46556.

International Standard Book Number: 0-87793-689-7

Cover and text design by Brian C. Conley

Printed and bound in the United States of America.

Contents

Introduction ... 7

Part I
The Profession of Faith (Creed) ... 9

Part II
The Celebration of the Christian Mystery (Liturgy and Sacraments) ... 35

Part III
Life in Christ (Morality) ... 59

Part IV
Christian Prayer ... 83

Note to the Catechist ... 95

Introduction

Part of your exercise of journeying in the Catholic faith is to uncover the deep treasures of Church teaching and tradition.

In earlier generations, Catholics and those preparing to receive the faith learned the essentials of their faith by reading and memorizing questions and answers from a Catholic catechism. The word *catechism* comes from a Greek word that means "to teach by word of mouth." More commonly, a catechism refers to a manual that gives basic instruction in a subject, usually by rote or repetition.

Questions of Faith reclaims some of that tradition and asks you to do a thorough study of the Catholic faith by reading and distilling answers from any suitable reference source, most suitably the *Catechism of the Catholic Church*.

In addition to the 160 writing questions, *Questions of Faith* also includes personal thought questions. The personal thought questions are intended to help you make a connection between what has been taught about faith in the Church's long, living tradition and your own experiences.

The hope of this book is that you use it to summarize for yourself some essential parts of Catholic doctrine and teachings. Through the research and writing of your own answers, not only will you have a written summary of the faith, but the summary will be in your own words and will be your own.

How to Use This Book

The *Catechism of the Catholic Church* is divided into four pillars, or parts, to form a whole. In simple terms, the *Catechism* covers the articles of Catholic creeds, sacraments, Christian living, and prayer. But the *Catechism* cannot be taken in simple terms. It is a thorough summary of faith and doctrine drawing on the sacred scriptures and two thousand years of tradition summarized in teachings and writings beginning with the Church fathers. *Questions of Faith* has been arranged in the same way, divided into four parts. To answer the questions in this book you will need either the *Catechism of the Catholic*

Church itself or one of many other popular catechisms. Each question in *Questions of Faith* is referenced both to paragraph numbers in the *Catechism* and to page numbers in *This Is Our Faith (TIOF)*, a catechism written by Michael Pennock and published by Ave Maria Press.

Here are some further suggestions for answering the questions in this book:

1. Read the question carefully. Make sure you understand what it is asking you.
2. Read the entire selection of cited paragraphs from the *Catechism* or other source.
3. Note the place in your reference that seems to provide the best summary for answering the question. Reread that section.
4. Based on what you've read, write your own answer summary in the space provided. Use complete sentences, proper grammar, and correct spelling as you are able. Write or print neatly so that you can easily refer to your own answers again.

PART I

THE PROFESSION OF FAITH

Creed

What if you put the clause "How are you able to . . . " before each of the creedal statements you recite each week at Mass? For example, instead of answering, "Do you believe in God?" answer, "How are you able to believe in God?" Or:

> How are you able to believe in Jesus Christ?
> How are you able to believe in the Holy Spirit?
> How are you able to believe in the Catholic Church? in the communion of saints? in the resurrection of the body? in everlasting life?

The answer to the "how are you able to" part of the question involves *faith*.

Faith is the name for a response to God. It involves a search as you make your way along looking for the meaning of life. Faith not only helps you answer, "I do believe," when you are asked, it also helps you to answer for yourself what and why you believe.

As you search, God reveals himself and gives himself to you.

Faith is your response to God's revelation.

The Church's faith is professed in its creeds. The Church has two primary creeds: the Apostles' Creed and the Nicene Creed. The Apostles' Creed developed from the beliefs of the early Christian community. The Nicene Creed was issued at the Church Council in Nicaea in 325.

This section asks you questions related to your search for God, God's disclosure of himself to you, and your own faithful response as stated in the Church's creeds.

Questions of Faith

1. What does it mean to say "I believe" or "we believe"? How do we witness the Church's faith? (*CCC* 26) (*TIOF* pp. 19-20)

- Who or what do you believe in more than anything else?

2. What are the ways we can come to know God? (*CCC* 31-35) (*TIOF* pp. 21-22)

Let us learn to cast our hearts into God.
—St. Bernard

- Describe a way you have come to approach God.

The Profession of Faith

3. **WHAT ARE THE STAGES OF GOD'S REVELATION TO HUMANKIND? BRIEFLY DESCRIBE EACH STAGE.** (*CCC* 54-67) (*TIOF* p. 24)

> *In times past, God spoke in partial and various ways to our ancestors through the prophets; in these last days, he spoke to us through a son. . . .*
>
> —Hebrews 1:1-2

• From what you know of the God of the Old Testament, how do you imagine God? How does coming to know Jesus allow you to better know God?

4. **WHAT IS MEANT BY APOSTOLIC TRADITION?** (*CCC* 75-83) (*TIOF* pp. 24-25)

• What are some ways traditions are handed on in your family?

5. **What is the relationship between Tradition and sacred Scripture? Why must they both be accepted by Catholics?** (*CCC* 80-82) (*TIOF* pp. 24-25)

• What are two modes for transmitting the truths of your country? the truths of your family?

---

6. **To whom did the Apostles pass on our heritage of faith? Who in the Church has authority to interpret God's Word in the form of Scripture and Tradition?** (*CCC* 84-87) (*TIOF* pp. 24-25)

And whoever rejects me rejects the one who sent me.
—Luke 10:16

• Jesus said to his apostles, "Whoever listens to you, listens to me" (Luke 10:16). How do these words help you to understand the Church's teaching authority?

The Profession of Faith

7. WHAT ARE DOGMAS OF THE FAITH? WHAT IS THE PURPOSE OF DOGMAS? (*CCC* 88-90) (*TIOF* p. 55)

> *Happy those whose words come from the Holy Spirit and not themselves.*
>
> —St. Anthony of Padua

• Name at least three unchanging truths that form the cornerstone of your life.

---

8. HOW IS THE CHURCH ABLE TO GROW IN THE FAITH? EXPLAIN HOW THESE WAYS CAN BE DESCRIBED AS SACRED TRADITION, SACRED SCRIPTURE, OR THE TEACHING OF THE MAGISTERIUM. (*CCC* 94-95) (*TIOF* p. 25)

• Who is someone who has inspired your faith? What is something you have read that has helped your faith to grow? Explain.

QUESTIONS OF FAITH

9. WHY IS GOD TRULY THE AUTHOR OF SACRED SCRIPTURE? DOES THIS MEAN THAT GOD ACTUALLY COMPOSED AND TRANSCRIBED THE WORDS OF THE SCRIPTURE? (CCC 101-108) (TIOF pp. 24-25; 30)

Pilate said to him, "What is truth?"

—John 18:38

• How do you think God inspired the authors of sacred Scripture in their writing? For example, was it through a dream? Or did God literally move their quills as they did the writing? Share your own idea.

10. WHAT ARE THREE CRITERIA FOR INTERPRETING SCRIPTURE IN ACCORDANCE WITH THE HOLY SPIRIT? (CCC 112-114) (TIOF pp. 24-25)

• What does it mean to take something "out of context"? How could this apply to misinterpreting Scripture?

The Profession of Faith

11. DEFINE "FAITH." HOW IS FAITH BOTH A GRACE AND A HUMAN ACT? (CCC 142-155) (TIOF p. 25)

> Lord, increase my faith. Help me to do your will. Amen.

- Describe a time someone shared his or her faith with you through words. Describe another time someone shared his or her faith with you through actions.

12. WHY IS FAITH MORE THAN AN ISOLATED ACT? (*CCC* 166-175) (*TIOF* pp. 25-26)

- What does it mean to "share your faith"? Who is someone you have shared your faith with? How did you do it? What happened?

QUESTIONS OF FAITH

13. WHAT IS THE MEANING OF THE WORD "CREED"? WHICH TWO CREEDS OCCUPY A SPECIAL PLACE IN THE CHURCH? WHAT DO THE THREE DISTINCT PARTS OF THE CREED SPEAK OF? (*CCC* 185-197) (*TIOF* p. 17)

> *Whoever says "I believe" says "I pledge myself to what we believe."*
> —Catechism of the Catholic Church 185

• Which article of either the Apostles' Creed or Nicene Creed do you have the most trouble understanding or believing? What is a question or statement that expresses your doubts?

14. HOW DO BOTH THE OLD TESTAMENT AND NEW TESTAMENT AFFIRM THAT THERE IS ONE GOD? (*CCC* 198-221) (*TIOF* pp. 31-32)

> *YHWH means "I Am Who I Am."*

• Imagine Yahweh spoke to you as he spoke to Moses. What would be one question you would ask him?

The Profession of Faith

15. **What are four implications of believing in one God?** (*CCC* 222-227) (*TIOF* pp. 41-42)

• Concretely, how have you lived each of the implications (listed above) of believing in one God?

16. **What is the Most Holy Trinity? Why is the Most Holy Trinity the central mystery of Christian faith and life?** (*CCC* 232-260) (*TIOF* pp. 34, 87-95)

> *The faith of all Christians rests on the Trinity.*
> —St. Caesarius

• What has God made known to you about the Trinity? How would you explain your understanding of the Trinity to a young child?

Questions of Faith

17. **How is God the Almighty?** (*CCC* 268-274) (*TIOF* p. 33)

• How does God's omnipotence have bearing on your life?

18. **What are some elements of the mystery of creation?** (*CCC* 295-301) (*TIOF* p. 35)

> *If God had drawn the world from pre-existent matter, what would be so extraordinary in that?*
> —St. Theophilus

• How do people share in God's creation?

The Profession of Faith

19. WHAT IS MEANT BY DIVINE PROVIDENCE? WHAT IS MEANT BY PHYSICAL AND MORAL EVIL? HOW DOES AN UNDERSTANDING OF DIVINE PROVIDENCE HELP TO EXPLAIN THE PRESENCE OF PHYSICAL AND MORAL EVIL IN THE WORLD? (*CCC* 295-314) (*TIOF* pp. 35-36)

- What is an example from your own life where God was able to bring good from something bad?

20. WHAT IS MEANT BY THE EXPRESSION "HEAVEN AND EARTH"? (*CCC* 325-327) (*TIOF* pp. 35, 157)

- How do you imagine heaven?

Questions of Faith

Holy Michael the Archangel, defend us in battle. Be our protection against the wickedness and snares of the devil. May God rebuke him, we humbly pray, and do thou, O Prince of the heavenly host, by the power of God, thrust into hell Satan and all wicked spirits who wander through the world for the ruin of souls.

21. **WHO ARE ANGELS? WHAT DO ANGELS DO?** (*CCC* 328-336) (*TIOF* p. 39)

- How do you imagine angels?

22. **WHAT DOES IT MEAN TO BE A PERSON MADE IN THE IMAGE OF GOD?** (*CCC* 356-361) (*TIOF* p. 35)

- Name at least three of your God-like qualities.

23. DEFINE "BODY" AND DEFINE "SOUL." EXPLAIN THE UNITY BETWEEN THE TWO. (*CCC* 362-368) (*TIOF* p. 35)

> *Surely nothing is too much for God when there is a question of sanctifying a soul.*
>
> —St. Vincent de Paul

- Apply your definition of the unity between body and soul to why the Church believes that human life begins at conception.

24. HOW DOES THE DOCTRINE OF ORIGINAL SIN HELP TO ANSWER THE QUESTION "WHERE DOES EVIL COME FROM?" (*CCC* 385-412) (*TIOF* pp. 36-37)

> *I sought whence evil comes and there was no solution.*
>
> —St. Augustine

- St. Thomas Aquinas taught that God permits evil in order to draw forth some greater good. Use an example from your own life to put this teaching into concrete terms.

QUESTIONS OF FAITH

25. EXPLAIN THE MEANING OF THESE NAMES AND TITLES FOR JESUS: JESUS, CHRIST, SON OF GOD, AND LORD. (*CCC* 430-451) (*TIOF* pp. 52-53)

• Sharing the Christian faith consists primarily in proclaiming Jesus Christ. Name at least three ways you do this.

26. WHY DID THE SON OF GOD BECOME MAN? IN OTHER WORDS, WHY DID THE WORD BECOME FLESH? (*CCC* 456-460) (*TIOF* p. 53)

Sacrifice and offering you did not desire,/but a body you prepared for me.

—Hebrews 10:5

• Name a situation you are aware of where a person of great power or esteem humbled himself or herself to raise the esteem of another.

The Profession of Faith

27. TRACE THE HERESIES SURROUNDING JESUS' TRUE DIVINITY AND TRUE HUMANITY. HOW DID THE COUNCILS OF EPHESUS, CHALCEDON, AND THE FIFTH ECUMENICAL COUNCIL AT CONSTANTINOPLE ANSWER THEM? (*CCC* 464-469) (*TIOF* pp. 54-56)

> *The Son of God . . . worked with human hands; he thought with a human mind. He acted with a human will, and with a human heart he loved. Born of the Virgin Mary, he has truly been made one of us, like to us in all things but sin.*
>
> —Gaudium et Spes (22§2)

- The Incarnation made Jesus one with humanity. In what ways are you just like Jesus?

28. WHAT DOES THE IMMACULATE CONCEPTION REFER TO? (*CCC* 490-495) (*TIOF* p. 141)

> *And coming to her, [the angel] said, "Hail, favored one! The Lord is with you."*
>
> —Luke 1:28

- What do you imagine that God has predestined for you?

QUESTIONS OF FAITH

29. HOW IS CHRIST'S WHOLE LIFE A MYSTERY OF REDEMPTION? OF RECAPITULATION? (*CCC* 514-518) (*TIOF* pp. 51-52)

• St. Irenaeus taught that "Christ procured a short-cut to salvation." What does his statement mean?

30. HOW DID JESUS SEEM TO BE ACTING AGAINST ESSENTIAL INSTITUTIONS OF THE CHOSEN PEOPLE, ACCORDING TO SOME JEWS? WHAT WERE JESUS' ACTUAL ACTIONS AND INTENTIONS IN THESE AREAS? (*CCC* 571-591) (*TIOF* pp. 65-66)

Jesus said: "Do not think that I have come to abolish the law or the prophets. I have come not to abolish but to fulfill."
—Matthew 5:17

• When was an occasion when you acted more out of ignorance than openness?

The Profession of Faith

31. **Who holds the greatest responsibility for Christ's death?** (*CCC* 595-598) (*TIOF* pp. 65-66)

• If Christ lived in your social setting, how would he be treated by you and your friends? Which peer group would he hang out with?

32. **How was Jesus' death part of God's plan of salvation?** (*CCC* 599-618) (*TIOF* p. 65)

> *Lord, by your cross and resurrection you have set us free.*
> *You are the savior of the world.*
>
> —Memorial Acclamation

• How do you participate in Christ's sacrifice? In other words, how do you pick up your own cross and follow him?

Questions of Faith

33. **What evidence is there that the resurrection of Christ is a real, historical event?** (*CCC* 638-646) (*TIOF* p. 68)

• Which type of evidence is most convincing to you of Christ's resurrection?

---

34. **What is the meaning and saving significance of Christ's resurrection?** (*CCC* 651-655) (*TIOF* p. 68)

• Describe the new perspective on life that Christ's resurrection brings to you.

The Profession of Faith

35. **Explain the events that must precede Christ's second coming.** (*CCC* 668-677) (*TIOF* pp. 69-70)

> Marana tha *means "Our Lord, come."*

- If a person tells you that we are living in the "last days" how should you respond? (Hint: see *CCC* 670)

---

36. **Who is the Holy Spirit?** (*CCC* 683-741) (*TIOF* pp. 73-80)

> *And no one can say, "Jesus is Lord," except by the holy Spirit.*
> —1 Corinthians 12:3

- Write a personal prayer directed to the Holy Spirit.

Questions of Faith

37. **Explain the Church's origin, foundation, and mission.** (*CCC* 758-769) (*TIOF* pp. 100-101)

The Church is like a great ship being pounded by the waves of life's stresses. Our duty is not to abandon ship, but to keep her on her course.
—St. Boniface

- What image best describes your vision of Church?

38. **Describe how the Church is the People of God, the Body of Christ, and the Temple of the Holy Spirit.** (*CCC* 781-801) (*TIOF* pp. 104-108)

- What are some ways that you detect Christ's presence in the Church?

The Profession of Faith

39. **What are things Christians can do to repair the unity of all Christians?** (*CCC* 820-822) (*TIOF* pp. 129-130)

• What is one effort you have taken or can take to repair Christian unity?

40. **How is the Church holy even though it is made up of sinners?** (*CCC* 823-829) (*TIOF* p. 121)

> *Just as water extinguishes a fire, so love wipes away sin.*
> —St. John of God

• Who is someone you know who fits the definition of holiness with imperfections?

Questions of Faith

41. Who belongs to the Catholic Church? (*CCC* 836-838) (*TIOF* p. 131)

The word catholic *means "universal" or "in keeping with the whole."*

• As an adult, how will you answer Christ's charge to "go and make disciples of all nations"?

42. How is Christ the source of the Church's ministry? (*CCC* 874-887) (*TIOF* p. 122)

• Who is a Church minister who has modeled servant leadership to you?

The Profession of Faith

43. **NAME AND DESCRIBE SOME VARIOUS EXPRESSIONS OF THE CONSECRATED LIFE.** (*CCC* 914-933) (*TIOF* pp. 335-336)

> *You only belong wholly to the world or wholly to God.*
>
> —St. John Vianney

• What do you find attractive about religious life? How can you imagine your life as a religious?

44. **WHAT DOES THE TERM "COMMUNION OF SAINTS" REFER TO?** (*CCC* 946-959) (*TIOF* p. 138)

• Sometimes those who have a near-death experience describe being greeted by a relative who has died. Who is a relative you think might greet you at the moment of death? Why?

Questions of Faith

45. How is Mary clearly the Mother of the Church? (*CCC* 963-972) (*TIOF* pp. 140-142)

And Mary said: "From now on will all ages call me blessed."

—Luke 1:48

• How is devotion to Mary different from adoration given to the Holy Trinity?

46. What are two ways the Church forgives sins? (*CCC* 976-983) (*TIOF* pp. 148-149)

• Why do you think the sacrament of Penance has been called a "laborious kind of baptism"?

The Profession of Faith

47. **What is meant by "rising" from the dead? Who will rise? How will they rise? When will they rise?** (*CCC* 997-1001) (*TIOF* p. 156)

> *There are both heavenly bodies and earthly bodies, but the brightness of the heavenly is one kind and that of the earthly another.*
>
> —1 Corinthians 15:40

- How do you imagine your heavenly body?

---

48. **What is the difference between the particular judgment and the last judgment?** (*CCC* 1021-1022, 1038-1041) (*TIOF* pp. 152-153)

- Do you have anything to fear of a fair judge?

Questions of Faith

49. DEFINE HEAVEN, PURGATORY, AND HELL. (*CCC* 1023-1037) (*TIOF* pp. 157-159)

> *How narrow the gate and constricted the road that leads to life. And those who find it are few.*
> —Matthew 7:14

- What do you have to do to go to heaven?

50. WHY DOES THE CHURCH END PRAYERS WITH "AMEN"? (*CCC* 1061-1063) (*TIOF* pp. 159-160)

- Do you believe everything you say you believe?

PART II

The Celebration of the Christian Mystery

Liturgy and Sacraments

Liturgy is a word that originally meant the "work of the people." More accurately, liturgy is our participation in the work of God.

What is the work of God? Primarily it is the work of Jesus Christ in bringing redemption to humankind and giving glory to God. Jesus' work was accomplished by the Paschal Mystery, that is, his passion, his resurrection from the dead, and his ascension into heaven.

In the liturgy, Christ's work remains present in our world today, and we have the opportunity to be active participants in his work. Liturgy is commonly associated with celebration because in fact we are celebrating the victory Christ won for us. We are also celebrating all of the statements of the creed in which we publicly proclaim our belief.

In liturgy—especially the eucharist and the other sacraments—we are able to proceed from what is visible to us (e.g., bread and wine) to the invisible; as the *Catechism* says, "from the sign to the thing signified, from the 'sacraments' to the 'mysteries'" (1075).

This section includes questions on how Jesus acts through the sacraments ("the sacramental economy") and other questions specifically about the seven sacraments and sacramentals. As you answer them, always keep in mind ways you can be active in the work of Christ.

Questions of Faith

51. **What is the meaning of liturgy in Christian tradition?** (*CCC* 1066-1075) (*TIOF* pp. 166-167)

> *To accomplish so great a work Christ is always present in his Church, especially in the liturgical celebrations.*
> —Sacrosanctum Concilium 7

• Name at least three things you did today to share in God's work.

---

52. **Explain the different ways the liturgy involves the Father, Son, and Holy Spirit.** (*CCC* 1077-1109) (*TIOF* pp. 167-168)

• How comfortable are you in giving all glory and honor to the heavenly Father?

The Celebration of the Christian Mystery

53. DEFINE "SACRAMENT." WHAT IS COMMON TO THE CHURCH'S SEVEN SACRAMENTS? (*CCC* 1113-1130) (*TIOF* pp. 168-169)

> *What else are the sacraments (all of them!) if not the action of Christ in the Holy Spirit?*
>
> —Pope John Paul II

• Share some signs of God's ongoing presence in your life.

54. WHO CELEBRATES THE LITURGY? HOW IS THE LITURGY CELEBRATED? WHEN IS THE LITURGY CELEBRATED? WHERE IS THE LITURGY CELEBRATED? (*CCC* 1136-1186) (*TIOF* pp. 173-176)

• Describe a liturgy that moved you emotionally, made you feel at home, or helped you to feel a part of the Church.

Questions of Faith

55. Why should the liturgy be celebrated with respect to many different cultures? (*CCC* 1200-1206) (*TIOF* p. 176)

• What cultures are represented in the celebration of liturgy at your parish or a neighboring parish?

56. What is the sacrament of Baptism? (*CCC* 1213-1216) (*TIOF* pp. 179-180)

The Greek baptizen *means to "plunge" or "immerse."*

• Explain why you would or would not choose to have a child of yours baptized.

The Celebration of the Christian Mystery

57. TRACE BAPTISM'S ROOTS IN THE OLD AND NEW TESTAMENTS. (*CCC* 1217-1228) (*TIOF* p. 180)

> *Or are you unaware that we who were baptized into Christ Jesus were baptized into his death?*
> —Romans 6:3

- Why do you think Jesus voluntarily submitted to Baptism?

58. HOW IS THE SACRAMENT OF BAPTISM CELEBRATED? (*CCC* 1229-1245) (*TIOF* pp. 182-185)

- What special features does your parish apply to the sacrament of Baptism?

QUESTIONS OF FAITH

59. BAPTISM IS NECESSARY FOR SALVATION. HOWEVER, GOD IS NOT BOUND BY HIS SACRAMENTS. PRACTICALLY, WHAT DOES THIS MEAN? (*CCC* 1257-1261) (*TIOF* pp. 186-187)

• Describe a real-life situation where you might have to choose to die for your faith.

60. WHAT ARE THE DIFFERENT EFFECTS OF THE SACRAMENT OF BAPTISM? (*CCC* 1262-1274) (*TIOF* p. 187)

Happy is our sacrament of water, in that, by washing away the sins of our early blindness, we are set free and admitted into eternal life!
—Tertullian

• How are you a different person because of Baptism?

The Celebration of the Christian Mystery

61. **HOW DO THE TRADITIONS OF THE SACRAMENT OF CONFIRMATION DIFFER BETWEEN THE EASTERN CHURCH AND WESTERN CHURCH?** (*CCC* 1289-1292) (*TIOF* pp. 188-189)

> *If anyone said, that the confirmation of those who have been baptized is an idle ceremony, and not rather a true and proper sacrament . . . let him be anathema.*
>
> —Council of Trent

- In your opinion, should the emphasis on the sacrament of Confirmation be more on Christian initiation or Christian maturity? Explain.

---

62. **WHAT ARE THE SIGNS IN THE RITE OF CONFIRMATION?** (*CCC* 1293-1296) (*TIOF* pp. 190-191)

- How does your life "give off the aroma of Christ"?

Questions of Faith

63. **What are the effects of the sacrament of Confirmation?** (*CCC* 1302-1305) (*TIOF* p. 188)

• What are some daily challenges you face that threaten your faith?

64. **Who can receive the sacrament of Confirmation? Who can confer the sacrament of Confirmation?** (*CCC* 1306-1314) (*TIOF* p. 189-191)

Age of body does not determine age of soul.
—St. Thomas Aquinas

• Who would (did) you choose to be your Confirmation sponsor? Why?

The Celebration of the Christian Mystery

65. Briefly define "Eucharist." List and explain some of the names for the sacrament of Eucharist. (*CCC* 1324-1332) (*TIOF* p. 196)

> *In a word, this sacrament is the very soul of the Church.*
> —Pope Leo XIII

• Which name for Eucharist best describes how you feel about the Eucharist?

---

66. What is at the heart of the Eucharistic celebration? (*CCC* 1333-1336) (*TIOF* p. 197)

• Jesus said, "Whoever eats my flesh and drinks my blood has eternal life, and I will raise him on the last day" (John 6:54). Many disciples found this saying too hard and left Jesus. What will you do?

67. **OUTLINE THE MAJOR MOVEMENTS OF THE MASS.** (*CCC* 1345-1355) (*TIOF* pp. 200-203)

• What active part have you already taken in the celebration of Eucharist? What part would you like to have in the future?

68. **HOW IS THE EUCHARIST A SACRIFICE?** (*CCC* 1359-1372) (*TIOF* pp. 198-199)

I simply ask you to remember me at the Lord's altar wherever you are.

—St. Monica to her son, St. Augustine, just prior to her death

• We Christians, though many, are one in the body of Christ. What does this statement mean to you?

The Celebration of the Christian Mystery

69. **HOW IS CHRIST TRULY PRESENT IN THE EUCHARIST?** (*CCC* 1373-1381) (*TIOF* p. 199)

• How you would explain Christ's presence in the consecrated bread and wine to a young child? a non-Catholic? a non-Christian?

---

70. **NAME SIX FRUITS OF HOLY COMMUNION.** (*CCC* 1391-1401) (*TIOF* pp. 204-205)

> *How sweet, the presence of Jesus to the longing harassed soul.*
> —St. Elizabeth Ann Seton

• How do you feel when you receive communion? What effect does receiving communion have on the rest of your day? the rest of your week?

Questions of Faith

71. **What is the purpose of the two sacraments of healing: Penance and the Anointing of the Sick?** (*CCC* 1420-1421) (*TIOF* pp. 215, 219)

If we say, "We are without sin," we deceive ourselves, and the truth is not in us.
—1 John 1:8

- What is the worst suffering or illness you have experienced?

72. **List and explain the various names for the sacrament of Penance.** (*CCC* 1423-1424) (*TIOF* p. 210)

- What do you recall about your own first Penance?

The Celebration of the Christian Mystery

73. WHY IS THE SACRAMENT OF RECONCILIATION NEEDED SINCE A PERSON'S SINS ARE FORGIVEN AT BAPTISM? (*CCC* 1425-1426) (*TIOF* p. 210)

And this sacrament of penance is, for those who have fallen after baptism, necessary unto salvation; as baptism itself is for those who have not been regenerated.

—Council of Trent

- Name a time you were given a second chance.

---

74. WHAT IS MEANT BY "INTERIOR REPENTANCE"? (*CCC* 1430-1433) (*TIOF* p. 211)

- When was an occasion when you had a change of heart and looked at a person or situation in a new way?

QUESTIONS OF FAITH

75. **NAME AND EXPLAIN EACH OF THE THREE REQUIRED ACTS OF THE PENITENT.** (*CCC* 1450-1460) (*TIOF* pp. 213-214)

To sin is human, but to persist in sin is devilish.
—St. Catherine of Siena

• Which act of the penitent do you typically find the most difficult to fulfill?

76. **EXPLAIN THE PRIEST'S ROLE AS MINISTER OF THE SACRAMENT OF RECONCILIATION.** (*CCC* 1461-1467) (*TIOF* p. 214)

• Do you have a particular confessor you prefer to go to for the sacrament of Reconciliation? Why or why not?

The Celebration of the Christian Mystery

77. What are the effects of the sacrament of Reconciliation? (*CCC* 1468-1470) (*TIOF* p. 215)

- Describe how you experience a "spiritual resurrection" after celebrating the sacrament of Reconciliation.

78. What are the elements of the sacrament of Penance? (*CCC* 1480-1484) (*TIOF* pp. 214-215)

> [Jesus] said to the paralytic, "Child, your sins are forgiven."
> —Mark 2:5

- What is your favorite story of forgiveness from the gospels?

Questions of Faith

79. WHAT DID CHRIST DO ABOUT SUFFERING AND ILLNESS? WHAT DOES HE CHARGE THE CHURCH TO DO? (*CCC* 1503-1510) (*TIOF* pp. 216-217)

God measures out affliction to our need.
—St. John Chrysostom

- What good can come out of suffering?

80. WHO CAN RECEIVE THE ANOINTING OF THE SICK? WHO CAN ADMINISTER THE SACRAMENT? (*CCC* 1514-1516) (*TIOF* p. 219)

- Describe a situation when you encouraged or would encourage a friend or family member to receive the sacrament of the Anointing of the Sick.

The Celebration of the Christian Mystery

81. HOW IS THE SACRAMENT OF THE ANOINTING OF THE SICK CELEBRATED? (*CCC* 1517-1519) (*TIOF* p. 218)

> *Is anyone among you suffering? He should pray.*
> —James 5:13

- What is your favorite gospel healing story?

---

82. NAME AND EXPLAIN THE EFFECTS OF THE SACRAMENT OF THE ANOINTING OF THE SICK. (*CCC* 1520-1523) (*TIOF* p. 219)

- How has an illness brought you or a family member closer to God?

QUESTIONS OF FAITH

83. WHAT IS VIATICUM? (*CCC* 1524-1525) (*TIOF* p. 217)

• Viaticum is described as the "seed of eternal life." Give one of your own descriptions.

84. WHAT IS THE DIFFERENCE BETWEEN THE PRIESTHOOD OF ALL BELIEVERS AND THE MINISTERIAL PRIESTHOOD? (*CCC* 1539-1553) (*TIOF* pp. 222-223)

The LORD has sworn and will not waver: "Like Melchizedek you are a priest forever."
—Psalm 110:4

• How have you experienced Jesus represented in the life of a priest you know?

The Celebration of the Christian Mystery

85. NAME AND EXPLAIN THE DEGREES OF ORDINATION. (*CCC* 1554-1571) (*TIOF* pp. 224-225)

• Who is your local bishop? What do you know about him?

86. WHAT IS THE ESSENTIAL RITE OF THE SACRAMENT OF HOLY ORDERS? (*CCC* 1572-1580) (*TIOF* p. 226)

• How would you encourage a teenage boy you thought would make a good priest to explore this vocation?

87. **What are the effects of the sacrament of Holy Orders?** (*CCC* 1581-1589) (*TIOF* p. 228)

• Name an important lesson or example of Christian living you have learned from a priest.

---

88. **How is God the "author of marriage"?** (*CCC* 1602-1617) (*TIOF* pp. 229-230)

> *The LORD God said: "It is not good for the man to be alone. I will make a suitable partner for him."*
> —Genesis 2:18

• Do you think God destines a husband and wife for each other?

The Celebration of the Christian Mystery

89. WHY DO SOME PEOPLE CHOOSE VIRGINITY FOR THE SAKE OF GOD'S KINGDOM? (*CCC* 1618-1620) (*TIOF* pp. 335-336)

• How are you willing to place your bond with Christ before all other bonds?

90. HOW IS A CATHOLIC MARRIAGE TYPICALLY CELEBRATED? (*CCC* 1621-1624) (*TIOF* pp. 232-233)

> *The state of marriage is one that requires more virtue and constancy than any other.*
> —St. Francis de Sales

• What was your favorite wedding you have ever attended? Why so?

Questions of Faith

91. **Who can be married in a Catholic wedding?** (*CCC* 1625-1637) (*TIOF* p. 233)

• What importance should a couple contemplating marriage put on having a compatible religious faith?

92. **What are the effects of the sacrament of Matrimony?** (*CCC* 1638-1642) (*TIOF* p. 235)

Father, you have made the union of man and wife so holy a mystery that it symbolizes the marriage of Christ and his Church.

—from the Rite of Marriage

• What does the statement "authentic married love is caught up in the divine" mean to you?

The Celebration of the Christian Mystery

93. How are children to be viewed in marriage? (*CCC* 1652-1654) (*TIOF* p. 235)

> *Perfect married life means the spiritual dedication of the parents for the benefit of their children.*
> —St. Thomas Aquinas

- What is one important life lesson you have learned from your parents?

---

94. What is meant by "domestic Church"? (*CCC* 1655-1658) (*TIOF* pp. 236-237)

> *The Second Vatican Council calls the family Ecclesia domestica, the "domestic Church."*

- Describe one incident of joy, love, or forgiveness present in your family in the past week.

QUESTIONS OF FAITH

95. DEFINE "SACRAMENTAL." NAME SOME SACRAMENTALS. (*CCC* 1667-1676) (*TIOF* pp. 176-177)

In the name of the Father, and of the Son, and of the Holy Spirit. Amen.

- What is a sacramental or devotional to which you are especially attracted? Why?

PART III

LIFE IN CHRIST

Morality

Being a Christian has parallels in the childhood game of "Follow the Leader." If you remember that game from when you were young, you had to do whatever the chosen leader did: stand on one foot, skip across the room, or wave your two hands in a silly fashion above your head.

At Baptism, we put on Jesus Christ and then participate in the life of the risen Lord. We follow him.

How do we do this? By imitating Jesus, who always did what was pleasing to God, his Father. This means living with an awareness that God is always with us, that our loving Father "sees in secret" (Mt 6:6) and has a desire for us to reach the perfection he created us for.

More concretely, we make the correct moral choices that lead us to our salvation.

We have been given several aids to help us choose what is right. In the Beatitudes, Jesus has provided us with a glimpse of the everlasting kingdom. We are blessed greatly when we do everything while acknowledging that we are children of God.

Our Church tradition has also provided us with a clear understanding of sin.

Also, the Decalogue, that is, the Ten Commandments of God's original covenant with the Hebrew people, states clearly for us what is required in the love of God and the love of neighbor—the great commandment expounded by Jesus.

The questions in this part will give you a clearer understanding of the aids offered for a Christian to choose what is right and good.

As St. Francis de Sales put it, "One of the most excellent intentions we can possibly have in all our actions is to do them because our Lord did them."

96. **What is unique about the human person in all of God's creation?** (*CCC* 1701-1709) (*TIOF* p. 244)

• How do you hear the voice of God urging you to "do what is good and avoid what is evil"?

97. **How do the Beatitudes respond to our natural desire for human happiness? What expressions characterize the Christian Beatitudes?** (*CCC* 1716-1724) (*TIOF* pp. 245-247)

> *No one is really happy merely because he has what he wants, but only if he wants things he ought to want.*
> —St. Augustine

• What do you find most difficult about living a life based on the Beatitudes?

Life in Christ

98. DEFINE "FREEDOM." WHAT IS THE PLACE OF HUMAN FREEDOM IN THE ECONOMY OF SALVATION? (*CCC* 1730-1742) (*TIOF* pp. 247-248)

> A bird can be held by a chain or by a thread, still it cannot fly.
>
> —St. John of the Cross

- Share one responsibility that comes with the gift of personal freedom.

99. NAME AND EXPLAIN THE THREE "SOURCES" OR CONSTITUTIVE ELEMENTS THAT DETERMINE THE MORALITY OF HUMAN ACTIONS. (*CCC* 1749-1754) (*TIOF* pp. 248-249)

- In what circumstances might a bad intention result in a good action? a good intention result in an evil action?

100. WHAT IS THE MEANING OF THE TERM "PASSIONS"? WHAT DO PASSIONS HAVE TO DO WITH MORALITY? (*CCC* 1762-1770) (*TIOF* pp. 249-250)

My heart and my flesh cry out/for the living God.
—Psalm 84:3

- How has one of your strong feelings led you to a good action?

101. WHAT IS CONSCIENCE? WHAT IS THE PURPOSE OF CONSCIENCE? (*CCC* 1776-1782) (*TIOF* p. 250)

- Recall an occasion from when you were younger of your conscience helping you to choose between right and wrong.

Life in Christ

102. **WHAT RULES IN MAKING A MORAL CHOICE APPLY IN EVERY CASE?** (*CCC* 1786-1789) (*TIOF* pp. 251-252)

• Put into your own words a general rule that can help you to make good and moral choices.

103. **NAME AND DEFINE THE FOUR CARDINAL VIRTUES.** (*CCC* 1803-1809) (*TIOF* p. 253)

> *The goal of a virtuous life is to become like God.*
> —St. Gregory of Nyssa

• What are some concrete efforts you can make to acquire the human virtues for your life?

QUESTIONS OF FAITH

104. NAME AND DEFINE THE THREE THEOLOGICAL VIRTUES. (*CCC* 1812-1829) (*TIOF* p. 254)

[God's] divine power has bestowed on us everything that makes for life and devotion, through the knowledge of him who called us by his own glory and power.
—2 Peter 1:3

• Share an example of how the theological virtues can help you in making a difficult moral decision.

105. WHAT ARE THE SEVEN GIFTS OF THE HOLY SPIRIT? WHAT ARE THE FRUITS OF THE HOLY SPIRIT? WHAT IS THEIR PURPOSE? (*CCC* 1830-1832) (*TIOF* pp. 254-255)

• Which gift of the Spirit do you need most in your life right now? Why?

Life in Christ

106. DEFINE "SIN." (*CCC* 1849-1851) (*TIOF* p. 255)

> *Sin is nothing else than to neglect eternal things and seek after temporal things.*
>
> —St. Augustine

• What do St. Paul's words, "Where sin increased, grace abounded all the more," mean to you?

---

107. WHAT IS AT THE ROOT OF ALL SINS? (*CCC* 1852-1853) (*TIOF* p. 255)

• What do you think would be the worst sin a person could commit? Why?

> *The time will come when there shall be one flock and one shepherd, one faith and one clear knowledge of God.*
> —St. Birgitta of Sweden

108. HOW IS PARTICIPATING IN SOCIETY NECESSARY FOR THE FULFILLMENT OF THE HUMAN VOCATION? (*CCC* 1878-1889) (*TIOF* p. 260)

- Name three ways you are an active participant in society.

109. WHAT IS MEANT BY THE "COMMON GOOD"? WHAT ARE ITS THREE ESSENTIAL ELEMENTS? (*CCC* 1905-1912) (*TIOF* pp. 261-262)

- What are some ways that human interdependence is increasing worldwide?

Life in Christ

110. **WHAT DOES RESPECT FOR THE HUMAN PERSON ENTAIL?** (*CCC* 1928-1933) (*TIOF* p. 262)

• Who is someone or some group of people you have difficulty calling "neighbor"?

111. **HOW ARE ALL PEOPLE ALIKE? HOW ARE PEOPLE DIFFERENT?** (*CCC* 1934-1938) (*TIOF* p. 264)

> *I tell you, to everyone who has, more will be given, but from the one who has not, even what he has will be taken away.*
> —Luke 19:26

• Why do you think that God did not choose to distribute "talents" equally?

112. How are divine law, natural moral law, the Old Law, and the Law of the Gospel—distinct expressions of the moral law—interrelated? (*CCC* 1950-1974) (*TIOF* pp. 276-277)

Alone among all animate beings, man can boast of having been counted worthy to receive a law from God.
—Tertullian

- Note how one civil or criminal law is an expression of the moral law.

113. What is meant by justification? How is a person's justification accomplished? (*CCC* 1987-1996) (*TIOF* pp. 277-278)

- Finish this sentence: "The justification of one evil person is greater than . . . ."

Life in Christ

114. DEFINE "GRACE" AND THE VARIOUS TYPES OF GRACE (E.G., SANCTIFYING GRACE, HABITUAL GRACE, ACTUAL GRACES, SACRAMENTAL GRACES). (*CCC* 1996-2005) (*TIOF* p. 278)

> God guides all by the action of his grace.
> —St. Anthony the Great

- Respond to the statement, "Everything is grace."

115. HOW DO WE HAVE MERIT IN GOD'S EYES? (*CCC* 2006-2011) (*TIOF* p. 279)

- St. Thérèse of Lisieux said that she wished to appear before God with "empty hands." What did she mean? What do you want to bring before God?

Questions of Faith

116. **Who are Christians who are called to perfection? How do they reach perfection?** (*CCC* 2012-2016) (*TIOF* p. 279)

> *You cannot be half a saint. You must be a whole saint or no saint at all.*
> —St. Thérèse of Lisieux

- Who is someone living or dead who meets the Christian understanding of perfection?

117. **What are the precepts of the Church? What is their purpose?** (*CCC* 2041-2043) (*TIOF* pp. 280-282)

- Why do you (or do you not) attend Sunday Mass?

118. **WHAT IS THE TRADITIONAL CATECHETICAL FORMULA OF THE TEN COMMANDMENTS? WHAT IS THE IMPORTANCE AND SIGNIFICANCE OF THE TEN COMMANDMENTS IN THE CHURCH'S TRADITION?** (*CCC* Section 2 Introduction, 2052-2074) (*TIOF* pp. 282-283)

• How do the Ten Commandments play a part in your moral decision-making? Give a concrete example.

119. **WHAT ARE SOME WAYS THAT THE FIRST COMMANDMENT EMBRACES FAITH, HOPE, AND CHARITY?** (*CCC* 2083-2094) (*TIOF* p. 286)

> *I. I am the Lord your God: you shall not have strange Gods before me.*

• What are some other gods you have directed your faith, hope, and love toward? What was the result?

QUESTIONS OF FAITH

120. NAME SOME BELIEFS AND PRACTICES CONDEMNED BY THE FIRST COMMANDMENT. HOW ARE THESE CONTRARY TO HONORING THE ONE, TRUE GOD? (*CCC* 2110-2128) (*TIOF* pp. 286-287)

• Which offense against the first commandment is most common among your peer group? What forms has it taken?

121. WHAT ARE SOME WAYS THAT GOD'S NAME IS ABUSED? (*CCC* 2142-2155) (*TIOF* p. 291)

II. You shall not take the name of the Lord your God in vain.

• How do you respond to someone who uses God's name in vain in your presence?

Life in Christ

122. **Why is the Christian's name important?** (*CCC* 2156-2159) (*TIOF* p. 292)

• What are the origins of your name? Who is your patron saint?

123. **For Christians, why does Sunday replace the sabbath of the "seventh day"?** (*CCC* 2175-2176) (*TIOF* pp. 292-294)

III. Remember to keep holy the Lord's day.

• Recall a special Sunday when you felt God's presence and had a glimpse of heaven.

124. WHAT ARE THE THREE REQUIREMENTS OF THE SUNDAY OBLIGATION? (*CCC* 2177-2188) (*TIOF* pp. 293-294)

• Name three actions you consider inappropriate for Sunday, and three you consider appropriate.

125. WHAT ARE THE DUTIES OF CHILDREN TO THEIR PARENTS? WHAT ARE THE DUTIES OF PARENTS TO THEIR CHILDREN? (*CCC* 2197-2206) (*TIOF* pp. 298-299)

IV. Honor your father and your mother.

• What's the best piece of advice ever given to you by your parents?

126. RELATED TO THE FOURTH COMMANDMENT, WHAT ARE THE DUTIES OF CIVIL AUTHORITIES TO CITIZENS? (*CCC* 2207-2213) (*TIOF* pp. 297-300)

• Describe a situation when your conscience could legitimately lead you to disobey the civil authorities.

127. WHEN IS KILLING MORALLY JUSTIFIED? OPPOSITELY, HOW ARE INTENTIONAL HOMICIDE, ABORTION, EUTHANASIA, AND SUICIDE SINFUL? (*CCC* 2258-2283) (*TIOF* pp. 300-301)

V. You shall not kill.

• Recall a murder of local or national prominence that impacted your life.

Questions of Faith

128. WHAT ARE SOME WAYS CHRISTIANS SHOW RESPECT FOR THE DIGNITY OF PERSONS? (*CCC* 2284-2301) (*TIOF* p. 303)

• How does your society and peer group falsely promote the "cult of the body"?

129. WHAT ARE THE TRADITIONAL ELEMENTS FOR THE MORAL LEGITIMACY OF WAR LAID OUT IN THE "JUST WAR" DOCTRINE? (*CCC* 2307-2309) (*TIOF* pp. 271-272)

Let us offer each other the sign of peace.

—From the Sign of Peace at Mass

• What are some questions you would ask your government leaders if you were called to serve in an armed conflict?

Life in Christ

130. **WHAT IS CHASTITY? WHAT DOES CHASTITY DEMAND OF THE INDIVIDUAL?** (*CCC* 2337-2347) (*TIOF* p. 304)

> *VI. You shall not commit adultery.*

• Describe a new friendship and an old friendship that are meaningful to you.

131. **WHAT ARE THE VARIOUS FORMS OF CHASTITY? WHAT ARE SOME OFFENSES AGAINST CHASTITY?** (*CCC* 2348-2359) (*TIOF* pp. 304-306)

• How strong is the commitment to saving sex until marriage among your peers?

QUESTIONS OF FAITH

132. WHAT IS THE PURPOSE OF SEXUALITY IN MARRIAGE? WHAT ARE THE OFFENSES AGAINST THE DIGNITY OF MARRIAGE? (*CCC* 2366-2391) (*TIOF* pp. 306-309)

• What are three qualities you hope for in a spouse?

133. IN WHAT WAYS DOES THE SEVENTH COMMANDMENT CALL FOR THE RESPECT OF THE GOODS OF OTHERS? RESPECT FOR THE INTEGRITY OF CREATION? (*CCC* 2407-2418) (*TIOF* pp. 309-311)

VII. You shall not steal.

• How is cheating on a school assignment or work project an offense against the seventh commandment?

Life in Christ

134. OF WHAT IS THE CHURCH'S SOCIAL TEACHING COMPRISED? WHY DOES THE CHURCH GIVE PREFERENTIAL LOVE FOR THE POOR? (*CCC* 2419-2449) (*TIOF* pp. 263, 269-270)

• Who is a neighbor in your community in need of your love and care? How will you respond?

135. WHAT IS TRUTH? HOW DO CHRISTIANS BEAR WITNESS TO THE TRUTH? (*CCC* 2464-2474) (*TIOF* pp. 311-312)

VIII. You shall not bear false witness against your neighbor.

• What does Jesus' teaching about truth—"Let what you say be simply 'Yes' or 'No'"—mean to you?

136. NAME SEVERAL OFFENSES AGAINST THE TRUTH. (*CCC* 2475-2487) (*TIOF* p. 312)

• What was an occasion when a lie you told did damage to another? How did you repair this injustice?

137. WHAT DOES "CONCUPISCENCE" REFER TO? HOW DOES A PERSON ACHIEVE PURITY OF HEART? (*CCC* 2514-2519) (*TIOF* pp. 304-305)

IX. You shall not covet your neighbor's wife.

• Who is a person you know or know of who best meets the description of "pure of heart"?

Life in Christ

138. **WHAT ARE FORMS OF MODESTY? HOW DOES MODESTY PROTECT THE INTIMATE CENTER OF A PERSON?** (*CCC* 2520-2527) (*TIOF* pp. 304-305)

• If you were instructing a young child in modesty how would you do it?

139. **WHAT DOES THE TENTH COMMANDMENT FORBID?** (*CCC* 2534-2540) (*TIOF* pp. 309-311)

X. You shall not covet your neighbor's goods.

• What do you think Jesus meant when he said, "For where your treasure is, there your heart will be also"?

QUESTIONS OF FAITH

140. WHAT IS TRUE HAPPINESS? HOW DOES THE DETACHMENT FROM WORLDLY RICHES LEAD TO ENTRANCE INTO THE KINGDOM OF HEAVEN? (*CCC* 2544-2550) (*TIOF* p. 311)

Eternity, eternity, when shall I come to you at last?
—St. Elizabeth Ann Seton

- If you meet God face to face, what will you do? What will you say?

PART IV

CHRISTIAN PRAYER

Prayer is the perfect conclusion to the *Catechism*.

Part I was concerned with the profession of faith, the actual statements of what we believe.

Part II showed how we celebrate all we believe, especially in the sacramental liturgy.

Part III reminded us that we must live out what we believe by making good and moral choices.

Naming our beliefs, celebrating our beliefs, and living our beliefs are only accomplished when we have a personal relationship with the living God.

That personal relationship is through prayer, the subject of Part IV.

As a young child you may have learned that prayer is "a conversation with God." It is indeed that, but also something more, for prayer cannot be initiated by our own efforts in any way. Rather, humility is the foundation of prayer. Only when we humble ourselves will God grant us the grace to pray.

In the words of Søren Kierkegaard, "Prayer does not change God, but changes the one who prays."

This part examines our universal call to prayer, the example of great pray-ers, and types of prayer, before focusing on the articles of the prayer given to us by Jesus, the Lord's Prayer.

141. WHAT IS PRAYER? (*CCC* 2558-2565) (*TIOF* pp. 317-318)

Prayer is the wine which makes glad the heart of all.
—St. Bernard

- How do you think of prayer?

142. HOW ARE THE PSALMS THE "MASTERWORK OF PRAYER" IN THE OLD TESTAMENT? (*CCC* 2585-2589) (*TIOF* pp. 318-319)

- What is a familiar Psalm verse that speaks to you?

Christian Prayer

143. WHEN AND HOW DID JESUS PRAY? (*CCC* 2598-2606) (*TIOF* pp. 319-320)

• Name three times and places during the course of the day where you could practically and consistently pray.

144. HOW DOES JESUS TEACH US TO PRAY? WHAT CAN WE LEARN ABOUT PRAYER FROM MARY? (*CCC* 2598-2606) (*TIOF* pp. 320-321)

> *Lord, teach us to pray.*
> —Luke 11:1

• What is your favorite parable about prayer from the gospels?

QUESTIONS OF FAITH

145. NAME AND EXPLAIN THE FIVE FORMS OF PRAYER. (*CCC* 2623-2643) (*TIOF* pp. 321-323)

• Reflect on occasions when you have or could have used each of the forms of prayer described above.

---

146. WHAT ARE WAYS THE HOLY SPIRIT TEACHES THE CHURCH TO PRAY? (*CCC* 2650-2660) (*TIOF* p. 323)

Hope does not disappoint, because the love of God has been poured out into our hearts through the holy Spirit that has been given to us.
—Romans 5:5

• Name an event from yesterday or today that became a time for prayer.

Christian Prayer

147. HOW IS ALL PRAYER—INCLUDING PRAYERS MADE IN COMMUNION WITH MARY, THE MOTHER OF GOD—ALWAYS IN RELATION TO JESUS CHRIST? (*CCC* 2663-2679) (*TIOF* pp. 323-325)

• When you pray, how do you imagine God the Father?

148. HOW DO CATHOLICS LEARN TO PRAY? WHERE DO CATHOLICS PRAY? (*CCC* 2683-2691) (*TIOF* pp. 323-325)

> *When we pray, the voice of the heart must be heard more than the proceedings from the mouth.*
> —St. Bonaventure

• Who taught you to pray? What is your favorite place to pray?

QUESTIONS OF FAITH

149. NAME AND EXPLAIN THREE EXPRESSIONS OF PRAYER. (*CCC* 2697-2719) (*TIOF* p. 325)

• Which expression of prayer would you like more instruction in? Why?

150. WHAT ARE SOME DIFFICULTIES A PERSON COMMONLY FACES WHEN TRYING TO PRAY? (*CCC* 2725-2745) (*TIOF* p. 326)

If God has stripped you of the sense of his presence, it is in order that even his presence may no longer occupy your heart, but himself.
—St. Francis de Sales

• What is a way you are commonly distracted when praying? What can you do to overcome distractions?

Christian Prayer

151. **WHY CAN THE LORD'S PRAYER BE CALLED "THE SUMMARY OF THE WHOLE GOSPEL"?** (*CCC* 2761-2772) (*TIOF* pp. 326-327)

> *The Lord's Prayer is the most perfect of prayers.*
> —St. Thomas Aquinas

• Recall three different times besides Mass that you have prayed the Our Father.

152. **WHY ARE WE ABLE TO INVOKE GOD AS FATHER IN OUR PRAYER?** (*CCC* 2777-2793) (*TIOF* pp. 327-328)

• What characteristics of God the Father have you experienced in earthly parents?

QUESTIONS OF FAITH

153. **WHAT DOES "WHO ART IN HEAVEN" REFER TO?** (*CCC* 2794-2796) (*TIOF* p. 328)

> *"Heaven" could also be those who bear the image of the heavenly world, and in whom God dwells and tarries.*
> —St. Cyril of Jerusalem

• How do you live the way of being described by the name "heaven"?

154. **HOW SHOULD THE PETITION "HALLOWED BE THY NAME" BE UNDERSTOOD?** (*CCC* 2807-2815) (*TIOF* p. 328)

• How is God's name made holy in your life?

155. WHAT IS MEANT BY THE PETITION IN THE LORD'S PRAYER "THY KINGDOM COME"? (*CCC* 2816-2821) (*TIOF* pp. 328-329)

• Name two ways you are committed to bringing Christ's presence to the world.

156. HOW DOES THE PETITION "THY WILL BE DONE ON EARTH AS IT IS IN HEAVEN" EXPRESS THE FATHER'S ENTIRE WILL? (*CCC* 2822-2827) (*TIOF* pp. 328-329)

• When was an occasion you took time to discern God's will for you? What was the result of your discernment?

157. Explain each part of the petition "give us this day our daily bread" ("give us," "this day," and "daily"). (*CCC* 2828-2837) (*TIOF* p. 329)

• Which do you find easier: to work as if everything depends on you or to pray as if everything depends on God?

158. What makes the petition "and forgive us our trespasses as we forgive those who trespass against us" so astounding? How does the next petition "and lead us not into temptation" go the root of its meaning? (*CCC* 2838-2849) (*TIOF* pp. 329-330)

There is a certain usefulness to temptation.
—Origen

• Is there anything or anyone you imagine to be impossible to forgive?

159. **WHAT IS THE MEANING OF "EVIL" IN THE LAST PETITION OF THE LORD'S PRAYER? HOW ARE WE TO BE DELIVERED FROM THE EVIL ONE?** (*CCC* 2850-2854) (*TIOF* p. 330)

> *If God is for us, who can be against us?*
> —Romans 8:31

• Compose your own short prayer for deliverance from Satan.

160. **WRITE AND EXPLAIN THE MEANING OF THE FINAL DOXOLOGY OF THE LORD'S PRAYER.** (*CCC* 2855-2856) (*TIOF* pp. 327, 330)

• How confident are you in being able to say "Amen, I agree" to all of the petitions of the Lord's Prayer?

Note to the Catechist

This book serves as a companion for any high-school religion course or adult faith formation program as a way to review the main teachings of the Catholic Church.

The numbered questions in this book can be used in many different ways, including:

Homework About five questions at a time may be assigned. Questions can be assigned in order or randomly from the various sections in the book.

In-Class Study Assign one or two questions at each session. The questions can be assigned randomly or related to a particular theme being covered in the course (e.g., creation, Eucharist, prayer).

Review Games For example, have the participants sit in groups. Ask the questions orally. The first person in a group to give an answer gets one point. The person with the most points at a table wins. The game can be played as an open-book or closed-book game.

Memorization Ask the participants to summarize a written answer into one or two sentences. Assign the summations for memorization.

Testing Use some or all of the questions on a class test. Or, assign certain questions as a test to be completed at home or in class. Collect the books and grade the assigned text questions.

Evaluation

Writing answers to the numbered questions is not only a worthwhile writing exercise, it will help the course participants summarize important elements of the Catholic faith in their own words. Recommend basic standards of composition. Answers should be written in complete sentences. Proper grammar and correct spelling should also be encouraged, if not required.

The answers to the numbered questions can be found in the *Catechism of the Catholic Church*. Often it is necessary for participants to distill their answers from a number of *Catechism* references. The particular references are listed with each question. In addition, all of the questions are referenced to *This Is Our Faith* by Michael Pennock (Ave Maria Press, 1998).

Personal Thought Questions

With each numbered writing question is a personal thought question that helps the participants apply the represented Church teaching to their own lives.

There are several ways to use these questions, including the following:

Journal Entries The personal thought questions can be assigned for journal writing. Allow time in the session for writing or give as a homework assignment. Occasionally, ask the participants to share their entries with a partner, in a small group, or with the entire class. Do make sure the participants have the option to keep some or all of their entries private.

Small-Group Sharing The personal thought questions can be used as discussion starters. Ask the questions orally. Have the participants meet in small groups of four or five to share responses.

Individual Reflection Allow the participants to choose one or more questions to focus on privately. The reflection time may be part of a communal prayer service or individualized prayer time.